Vegetables from Stems and Leaves

MILLICENT E. SELSAM

PHOTOGRAPHS BY JEROME WEXLER

William Morrow and Company
New York 1972

Selsam, Millicent (Ellis) 1912–
    Vegetables from stems and leaves.

    SUMMARY: Explains the cultivation and growth of twelve
vegetables including onions, asparagus, cabbage, and lettuce.
    1. Vegetables—Juvenile literature. [1. Vegetables]
I. Wexler, Jerome, illus. II. Title.
SB324.S46   635   72–390
ISBN 0-688-20035-4
ISBN 0-688-30035-9 (lib. ed.)

The author and photographer thank
Dr. Howard S. Irwin,
Executive Director of the New York Botanical Gardens,
for checking the text and photographs of this book.

ACKNOWLEDGMENTS FOR PHOTOGRAPHS
John H. Gerard, National Audubon Society, 11
Ferry Morse Seed Company, 31, 35, 37 left, 41, 42 bottom
Northrup, King and Company, 33 top
Millicent E. Selsam, 8
United States Department of Agriculture, 27 bottom, 34 left, 38 right, 39, 42 top

ASPARAGUS

An asparagus plant
is growing from a seed
planted in the soil.

It is getting bigger.

3

Here is the same plant after one season's growth. The parts that appear to be fine, thin leaves are really tiny branches.

The top of the plant is feathery and looks almost like a fern. The bottom, underneath the ground, is made up of roots and buds. The roots and buds are called the "crown" of the asparagus plant.

Usually one-year-old crowns are planted in
the vegetable garden. But two to three years
pass before the crowns produce a good
asparagus crop. Here is an asparagus shoot,
which is called a "spear," growing from a
three-year-old crown. The spears grow quickly,
as much as four inches a day.

They are cut off when their length
reaches nine to ten inches, packed
in boxes, and shipped to market.

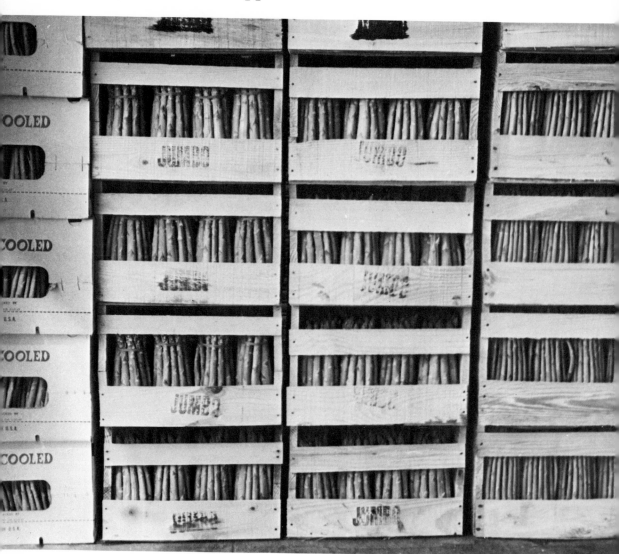

If left in the
ground, the spears
continue to grow.
Scales open and
expose branches.

The branches
grow rapidly.

In the picture
on the right
the branches are
opening further.

10

Now you can see how feathery the branches become.

11

Flowers form on the branches.

There are two kinds of asparagus plants. The first produces only male flowers like this one. Notice the stamens are full of pollen.

The second produces only female flowers. There is a part called the "pistil" inside this flower. The top of the pistil is called the "stigma." It is divided into three sections.

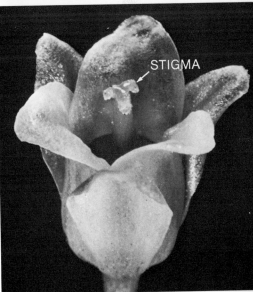

If you look into the female flower, you can see the bottom of the pistil. It is three parted and is called the "ovary." Inside the ovary are ovules.

The ovules can become seeds if they are
fertilized, or joined by the contents of
a pollen grain. In this picture you can see
an insect visiting an asparagus flower.
When it lands on the flower with stamens,
it gets dusted with pollen. When it flies
to the flowers with pistils, it accidentally
brushes the pollen grains onto the stigma.

The pollen grains send
out tubes, which grow
down to the ovary,
where the ovules are.
The contents of each
pollen tube join with
an ovule. Now the ovules
are fertilized and
change into seeds.
The ovary around the
ovules develops into
a fruit called a "berry."

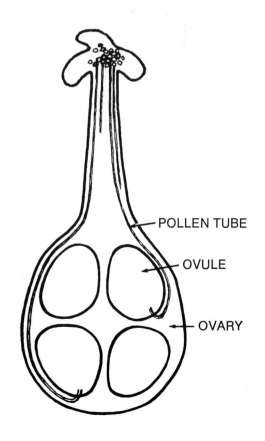

POLLEN TUBE

OVULE

OVARY

15

Here is an asparagus berry.

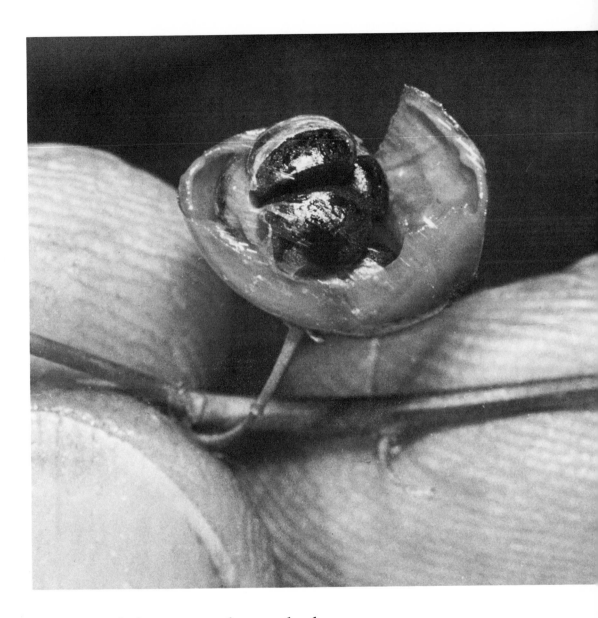

Inside each berry are the seeds that
can grow into new asparagus plants.

17

POTATOES

Potatoes do not usually grow from seeds.
Instead farmers plant small whole potatoes
or pieces of large potatoes. They are called "seed
potatoes." They can grow into new potato plants
because of their eyes, which are undeveloped
buds. You can see them on this whole potato.

18

Does this eye look like a human eye to you? Under the part that looks like an eyebrow you can find the buds.

When you put potatoes in a dark, moist place or plant them in the soil, the buds grow. First roots grow down into the soil.

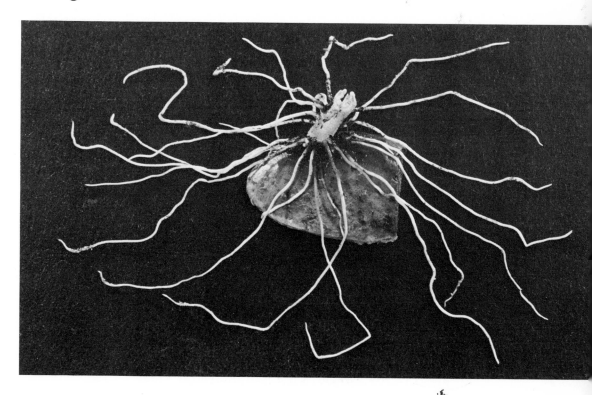

Then stems
and leaves
grow. A piece
of potato with
several eyes
was planted
in the pot.

The plant
grows bigger.

In the picture on the left the plant has been
knocked out of the pot, and you can see
that it is full of roots. You also can see small
potatoes forming. In the picture on the
right the soil has been washed away from the
part of the potato that is underground, and
you can see the small potatoes.

STOLONS

The potatoes are attached to underground stems
called "stolons." They creep sideways through
the earth. They are thick and fleshy compared to
the stringy roots. Here the roots have been
cut away so that you can see the stolons and the
potatoes that have formed at their tips.

22

This picture shows
how the potato
develops. The tip
of the stolon
starts to swell.

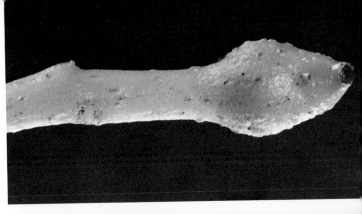

Slowly the swollen
parts get bigger
until they are
full-sized potatoes.

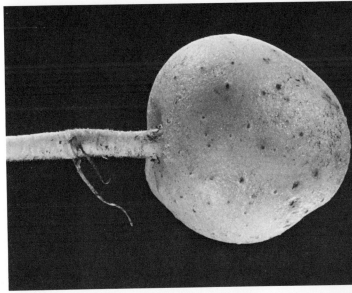

Here is the crop
from one potato plant.

23

Potato plants produce flowers, but few of them set seed from the flowers. Nobody tries to grow potatoes from seed. The easier, faster and surer method is to grow new plants from seed potatoes.

LETTUCE

A lettuce seed
is sprouting

The young plant
has a few leaves.

A few weeks after the seed has been planted
the lettuce leaves can be eaten. These heads of
lettuce are ready to be harvested.

There are
two main kinds
of lettuce.
The leaves of one grow in a tight head.
The leaves of the other are in a loose head.

27

If the lettuce
is not harvested
in time, the stem
gets longer and
small yellow
flowers appear.

The flowers look
like dandelions.
Each flower is
really a cluster
of tiny flowers.

After pollination by insects and fertilization, a seed forms in the ovary of each flower in the cluster. When an ovary ripens, it becomes a fruit. Each fruit has a single seed inside and a tiny parachute of soft hairs. A package of lettuce seed contains fruits without the parachutes. The parachutes are removed before they are packaged.

30

SPINACH

The leaves of this spinach
plant are ready to be eaten.

If the spinach is not harvested, it sends up stems carrying flowers, just as the lettuce plant does. Spinach is also like asparagus, for there are two kinds of plants. One produces only male flowers. The other produces only female flowers. In the picture on the left you can see the tiny female flowers clustered at the base of the leaves. When they are pollinated and fertilized, seeds develop in the ovaries of the female flowers.

When the seeds are planted, new spinach plants grow.

CABBAGE

The leaves of cabbage plants are eaten too.
Here a cabbage head has been cut through the
middle, and you can see that there is practically
no space on the stem between the leaves. The
leaves and the short stem make up one huge bud.

Toward the end of the growing season or during the next year the head breaks open. The stem grows out of the overlapping leaves and bears a lot of pretty yellow flowers.

From the flowers seeds develop, which grow into more cabbage plants like the one above just starting to grow.

MUSTARD

Have you ever eaten mustard greens?
Here is a mustard plant. Its leaves, which
are called "greens," are sharp and tangy.

35

If not picked at harvesttime, the stem gets long and bears flowers just as the lettuce plant does.

From the flowers come seeds. Here a crop
of mustard seed is ready to be harvested.

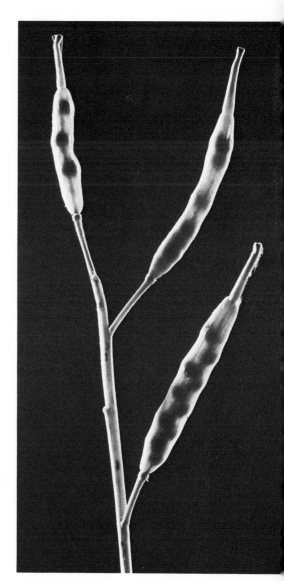

The fruit is a slender pod.
You can see the seeds inside.
Some kinds of mustard plants
have seeds that are crushed
to make the mustard used on
sandwiches and frankfurters.

FLESHY LEAVES

STEM

ONIONS

The onion is a bulb.
It is made up of a short
stem and closely packed
thick, fleshy leaves.

A large part of the
onion crop in the
United States is grown
from seed. But onions
also can be raised
from small bulbs
called "onion sets."

38

When the bulb develops, the fleshy leaves inside it grow out, becoming long, hollow, and green. Under the ground small bulbs get bigger till they are ready to be harvested. If full-grown bulbs are kept over the winter and planted in the spring, they send up stalks of flowers. The onion seed comes from the ovaries of the flowers after pollination and fertilization.

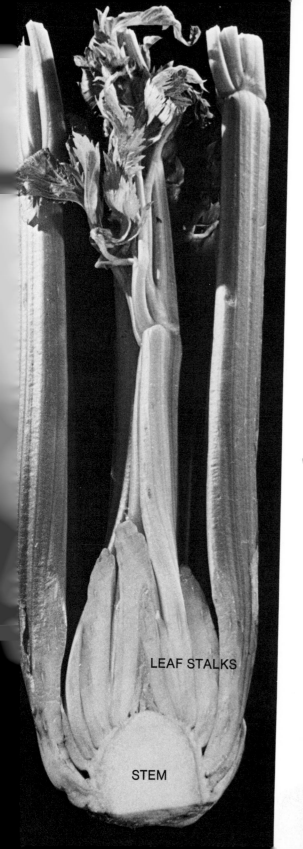

LEAF STALKS

STEM

CELERY

Here is the part of the
celery plant that we eat.
It is made up of fleshy
stalks of the leaves.
The leaves are used too,
to flavor soups and stews.

At the very bottom
of a bunch of celery
there is a stem from
which roots grow down
into the ground.

In order to get celery seeds to plant, the farmer must select some celery plants and keep them through the winter either in the fields or in cold storage. The following spring these plants become shrublike, growing two to three feet high with lots of flowers that resemble Queen Anne's lace. After pollination and fertilization, the seeds develop in the ovaries of the flowers.

KALE AND COLLARDS

Kale and collards are two more plants whose leaves are edible. Both kale and collards are a type of cabbage plant, but they do not form heads. Their leaves are used as a boiled green vegetable.

The leaves of several other plants provide pungent herbs with which to season food.

CHIVES

The leaves of chives are hollow and cylindrical. The underground part of the plant is made up of very small bulbs, which live from year to year.

The flowers are rose purple. From them come chive seeds. But people grow chives mostly from clumps of bulbs that they can buy in a vegetable store.

DILL

The dill plant is used to flavor pickles and salads and many other foods.

The flowers, like those of the celery plant, resemble Queen Anne's lace and are in the same family. From the flowers come the dill seeds, which are almost as common a flavoring as the leaves.

PARSLEY

Parsley is used most of all the herbs in cooking. Its leaves can be either curly or flat. It is a relative of celery and dill, and it also has flowers like Queen Anne's lace. They appear the second year of the plant's growth.

Can you think of any other vegetables that are either stems or leaves?

INDEX

BY THE SAME AUTHOR
Animals as Parents
The Carrot and Other Root Vegetables
The Courtship of Animals
How Animals Live Together
How Animals Tell Time
How to Grow House Plants
The Language of Animals
Maple Tree
Microbes at Work
Milkweed
Peanut
Plants That Heal
Plants That Move
The Plants We Eat
Play with Plants
Play with Seeds
Play with Trees
The Tomato and Other Fruit Vegetables
Underwater Zoos